kindness separates night from day

DESIGN & LAYOUT
Sandorf Passage

PUBLISHED BY
Sandorf Passage
South Portland, Maine, United States
IMPRINT OF
Sandorf
Severinska 30, Zagreb, Croatia
sandorfpassage.org

ORIGINALLY PUBLISHED BY SANDORF AS
Dobrota razdvaja dan i noć

COVER ART
Marina Uzelac

PRINTED BY
Kerschoffset, Zagreb

Sandorf Passage books are available to the
trade through Independent Publishers Group:
ipgbook.com / (800) 888-4741.

Library of Congress Control Number: 2023930598

National and University Library Zagreb Control Number:
001163852

ISBN: 978-9-53351-434-5

Co-funded by
the European Union

This book is published with financial support by
the Republic of Croatia's Ministry of Culture and Media.

Funded by the European Union. Views and opinions
expressed are however those of the author(s) only and do
not necessarily reflect those of the European Union or The
European Commission. Neither the European Union nor
the granting authority can be held responsible for them.

kindness separates night from day

marija dejanović

translated from the croatian by vesna maric

SAN-
DORF
PAS-
SAGE

SOUTH PORTLAND | MAINE

THE MOVE

the moving of our organism happened
overnight

we threw off our fleshy armor
and forgot how to feel burdened

this didn't bother us much

the body vibrates as it lies by the lake

a water lily grows out of its ears
and its spine is an arrow
pointing south

where do colors go
when petals fall and return to the soil's embrace?

into your nose

they go into your nose

PASSPORT

The first couple of months
I didn't speak
When I finally spoke, I couldn't stop

I found out about the difference between a sponge and a
lightbulb
learned grandma's words and created my own

I could talk about everything
except myself

That remained in place
for the first twenty years

*

My first words were *wha-dee*
uttered before a plate of bean stew
What's this?

There was no one around that morning
who might see themselves in those words
who might want to lie that my first word was *daddy*

My first words cheered up mostly me
Father was sad because he'd missed them
Mother was angry because they were a mark
of his absence

He worked in a different town to put food on our table
That's why he never ate with us
That's why we ate in silence
That's why he ate our silence upon his return

Mother sees him at the door and says
I wish you weren't back
What she meant was
I wish you'd never left

I wish no one had to leave
For such departures belong to those
who never wanted to go

They are the departures of those with nowhere to return

*

A shortage of home, too many apartments
The first five years in Bjelovar, Zagreb, and Sisak several
times

We arrived at Germany's doorstep, they didn't let us in
Despite my granddad saying I built those apartments

At university in Zagreb they asked me where I was from

I was in my birthplace
only at my birth
And over where I grew up I was always
the girl with a funny accent

All this was resolved when I went abroad
Where our accents all sounded the same

Now I leave only when I wish
And remain as long as I need to

If anyone wants to know the difference
between leaving and returning:

the difference is in me

*

He drinks a Greek drink, the same as the Croatian one
just triple
a nut mix always comes with the drink
a sign of hospitality

The first tree I ever saw here was an orange tree
the cities are so full of concrete they plant these fragrant
suns

If you look up a little, you'll see greenery hanging off the
balconies

The Greeks have these floating lawns and we have
gardens

That is why I joked that he was a bird
who lands on the balcony and pecks at the almonds

I need to have a garden
because I sit there and drink homemade elderflower
juice

Here, sunbathe, you lizard, he says
and points at the sea

*

Most of my childhood
I played football with the neighborhood boys
entirely like the other players
then my breasts grew

I could no longer remove my T-shirt
and pour water on my bare torso
when the sun baked the cars
on the cracked asphalt of the suburbs

the city's courtyard that sat so lonely
it accepted even us, even though it could hardly stand
itself
offered us a job and a place to live

What did I witness in that childhood?
A fight here and there, a cat having her litter
under the stairs

A hill covered in snow
tons of mud on the hill after the snow
then snowdrops sprouting

*

If I had wanted to travel from Sisak to Dubrovnik
I would have needed a passport

In my first twenty years
I only saw Dubrovnik
on *Game of Thrones*

*

I say, what's that
he says, tsipouro

The tourists think we drink ouzo
but ouzo is the swill the tourists drink

*

I don't like tourists
Big shopping centers usually follow in their wake
community leaves with them and a slave state takes over

He says tourists come to the beach in front of my house
and then I can't go out on my kayak
That beach is for him how that bit of the road was for me
where I used to play football
and the tourists are like cars

They pass by in loud numbers

They remind us that a space doesn't belong to us
even if it is where we spend our lives

They teach us that to own and to belong
are not one and the same thing

*

Historic men
and the few remembered women
are tourists in flip-flops on the Velebit of the world

They wrote either of friends, or the dead
That is why they decorated all truths
made them look more like lies

They remembered the things that could be retold
in the garden or on a balcony
photographed and stuffed in a pocket

taken along

*

In my youth I presented
an uglier version of what we are
myself and the world — but not my loved ones

I let them rest in silence

That silence was the best
I could give

Today I try to say it
exactly as I think it is

— remember who you are while there is still something
to remember
— a garden is bigger than a country

But still I catch some devils by their horns

— an evening that bites the face
— a lounge chair with an indelible stain

There are days I'd fight myself

Threw an axe onto the moon because it was shining
chased a train with a knife because it was running late

—people's flaws are most dangerous
when we mistake them for virtues—

I don't strike the weak even if they strike first   15

As I walk along the road
I am careful to remember all
the irrelevant things

AUBERGINE

You know, this is where I'm from now
mother told me while watching the half of the garden
that was full of aubergines she'd grown
with too much care, like children, on a small plot of land
she'd bought with hard-earned money
dug up laboriously left to right, upward
as if knitting a vest

The other half still has soil that needs digging
and it seems that with each wielding of the spade
she increases the distance between the village of her
childhood
and this yard in which we stand
as if each step forward is a new void
but that, also, each new void is a reason to move on
In each hole she plants a memory
of long-buried faces

Over there no longer exists
Although you'd only visited maybe twice in your life
and I have already been here a year longer
than I had spent in—
and she pauses before saying
I was born in the times of ethnic cleansing
but there had been nothing clean

in the hospital where I first appeared
—miraculously alive—
while the splayed flesh of my mother was surrounded by
dying soldiers and civilians

—her flesh—and that I was born in a bed
in which no woman should ever give birth
and no child ever meet the world
that such hospitalization cannot be called a service
but a crime against humanity

She lightly raised her elbow
to wipe the sweat off her brow with the back of her
hand
and to stop digging

We got into the car in silence
After several hours we saw the border police

She still doesn't like them

Just like the last time I saw her
granny wears a worn-out gray dress
and a wide smile

She stands at the gate, squinting

She's made potato pie for us

Although she has remembered nothing for years now
granny can still perfectly recall my mother's face

You haven't changed at all, daughter
She says, and reaching out her hand
strokes my cheek

STRAIGHT LINES

The yellow languor of the arrival
of the tree fruit, apples, pears
sprung from a stone dug in like a heel
swam out of the water

All fruit is yellow
and appears only in clues
The thickness of noon approaches us like a tame train
regularly, with gentle deviations
and warns that we must be cautious
soft of smiles, clean of surface
with a metal, warmed-up heart
ready to kill grass snakes with a hoe
our search leaving no stone unturned

She has fireproof hands
hides them in the stove like a snake hides its legs
cranes her neck, the nape and chin following straight
lines
Tracing small scars in the sky
released from the backside of the airplane

She cannot burn herself on me
she cannot find out my name
Our pupils are fixed, framed by eyelashes
that calibrate like buds
buds of May
seeing off legs and heads

I am so happy to have you
you stole a car part just so no one could drive it
and now you're hitchhiking, thinking why
did I need all of this

Your grassy tongue conceals lies
sweet summer alterations that make you love me more

When you melt my name in your mouth
I could swear it's a different name

When you kiss my cheek with your mouth
I could swear
it isn't my cheek

PUMPKIN PIE

A watermelon is a fish from a garden
she said and laughed

She had a wide-brimmed straw hat
and sat at the table in the yard

Her shoulders were sprinkled with freckles
and a knife shone in her hand

We have a watermelon, but who'll slaughter it
that's the expression in her village
as if it's about slicing a wound in the warmth

She said when you leave, who'll go for walks with me

She pressed her thumb against her cheek,
her index finger on her forehead
and released a small weary sigh after work

Said I'd like to make a pumpkin pie
but I can't eat it on my own

*

She mostly walks alone
Moves around the streets like a small flock

Her feet, like two fish
perennially in the shade and under the surface
invisible they carefully mark out
the blood flow of the world

Sugar collects in the veins on her legs
and all her shoes bother her, that's how much she walks

*

Thorns for my Sleeping Beauty
Cherry liquor for the sweetly acidic symbiosis

And the memory of that man, poor him
who had, when he heard we shared a name
asked if we were sisters

*

The sun levels out all kinds of cruelty
makes them less horrible

PRETTIER LULLABIES

Nature is simple—

—music appears in the touch of the hollow bones
of a bird and wind
and then it scatters

or resurrects toward the sun shaped as a bubble
from the open mouth of a fish

There is no passing from one world to another
There is no other world

People are the part of nature that spites nature
We say: there are two worlds

we complicate the music and the vanishing

*

I want you to play this song at my funeral
you said about a song we heard on the radio

it was a Wednesday and springtime

I remember that moment well
since then I see your every wrinkle even before it forms
since that day, every time you cough
I hear the sound of your lungs
even before your mouth opens

If you had become a singer, as you'd wished
I'd have retained memories
of objectively more beautiful lullabies

As it is, the lullabies were beautiful
because you were the one who had sung them

*

Now even that song is special
when I hear it, my chest turns heavy and I cry

Crying at bad songs makes me feel weak
and for this, as usual, I blame you

I hate this blame we share
because it blurs the boundary between you and me

Crying at the bad song makes me smaller
Forces me to curl up
and want a hug

It makes me lie that I am feeling ill

I wish to, like back then, hide to see
if you'll look for me
If you'll find me and tell me
that I'm too big for hiding

FOR ME, WHO DECIDED TO REMAIN THERE

There is a person who acted differently
She is living my life convinced it's her own

She sits on the sofa from which I got up
the morning I went to catch the plane
and is writing my book—
 —definitely not this one

A moment came for a choice
between habit and need
myself and myself

The decision was made
by your dark eyes
flared up by the draught in the room
when someone flung open
the doors and windows

Your eyes—two fireplaces
into which I dove gladly

Static and mobile
like a rocking chair

*

She calls up my friends sometimes
they tell her secrets unknown by me
she plans short trips with them
to places I haven't been

spring cleaning, coffee
and cake in the neighbourhood
many of the plans actually come to pass

She doesn't have two white cats
because she thinks she prefers dogs

Their loyalty, in theory
relieves her fear of abandonment

One day she will gather all my friends
and they will meet up

It won't be on the day of my departure

When this lovely pack forms
she will finally be ready
to adopt a dog

*

How beautiful is her solitude
when being observed

She's not aware of herself
that's why she's unshaken

*

I don't know how
or when
but one day

I will knock on her door
or she on mine

You will open it

You'll ask me where I've been

ON THE WAY TO THE SHOP

In a country where few speak your language
everyone speaks louder than you
everyone is more visible, more protected
hidden by numerousness
on the way to the tea shop you feel much too noticeable
The movements of your knees reflect your lack of friends

Your gait is stiff, too strict
and although everyone is extremely kind
they don't dig into your flesh out of the goodness of
their hearts
they talk amongst themselves not to bother you
they say good day and goodbye

Still, you feel like a pair of metal compasses
whose sharp shiny needle point stabs the concrete
meter after meter
As you walk from the flat to the shop, from the shop to
the flat
you leave behind a vanishing circle of your presence, a
language
of mutual incomprehension;

when you're buying tea from the friendly shopkeeper
it is you, rather than the dried leaves, that is on display

Returning from the shop you begin to resemble them
Aimless, you are an eye that envelops
and does not reveal

Out of love for yourself you don't question how you feel
just like out of your love for animals

you eat herbs planted by another's children
who will never be able to afford the food they grow
you buy cashew nuts in a plastic bag
whose production melts women's identity off their
fingertips

But those are some other women, somewhere far away
women whose sisters live in towns that topple onto their
heads
legal slave women

You have chosen your own hard times
Bought your good times with them

The streets are full of small shops
Each shop has many woven baskets
each woven basket holds a small personal defeat
You walk blonde, blue-eyed
because your skin is suntanned
it is lovely to see you in every street

If they speak to you in that language
you shrug under your hat

They could say they love you or curse you
and you wouldn't know the difference

this ignorance is your small personal victory

ABOUT THE EARTHQUAKE, FROM AFAR

One half of the building collapsed
Those walls had given my brother asthma

The other half was where
twenty years ago
a neighbor threw down his dog
and a couple of years later, himself too

In its corridors
I played with Barbies
and spat into watercolors
so I could paint the door to the yard
when I was home alone

I still believe
we didn't deserve the punishments
that came to us

In my gut I sense the bird that flies over
the ruined houses
the cracked beams
the weeping bicycles and the people's bent backs

They wade through their shared malaise
in pajamas and slippers
as if through deep waters

Upon reading
a childhood neighbor writing
that someone should finally knock down that old
building
because its bricks fall on the roof of their house
every time the earth shivers

something inside me falls like a brick
and goes silent

MY FRIENDS

My friends live in the spaces between a wardrobe and a
wall
impossible to reach

No matter how far I stretch my arms, a cobweb of
silence
enters my mouth; my friends are the dark silence of
whitewash
I tell her: choose a frame for the picture
and let the crown of your head
peek out through its empty body
the soft roots of your hair that the sun doesn't reach
sprinkled with flour

sneak out of his kitchen or jump out of the window
from the tenth floor
particles of possibility will catch you
like the neighborhood park ash flowers

Your eyes: symbols for swollen, heavy breasts
sagging from your father's gaze
horse milk and gifts
which are missing from your skin
unlike your husband's cruel lips

His words gather in your navel
across your belly they climb toward your neck
those words are cypresses from the graveyard

and suddenly, instead of dust
you're the one hanging off the ceiling light

My friends are mine because they are no one's
they only listen to themselves, touch themselves
and only cry by themselves
My friend is a table leg
whose splinter sticks the finger
while moving house

My friend: a small plastic sphere
filled with brown liquid

My friend is a curly hair
in the pipe of her throat

He tells her: we formed common boundaries
so that we could wipe down furniture together
She tells him: it's easy to fall apart, it's hard
to pin down a pea with a fork

My friends are the first sorrows
I could truly love

They will be the first to make decisions
and the only ones to see them through

My friends are tall buildings
clutching onto the foundations

My friends are an airplane
with cement legs

PHOTOGRAPH OF A DUCK

I photographed a duck
standing on a wooden stump
To show you the duck and the stump
Or to say: there was a duck
The rest of the day I apply makeup
and look at myself from a distance, until I recognize
myself
and then I wave to myself
I say
hello
in our language, to myself
When I finish up, I say: this is a mouth

or, such a mouth:
and I sink my lips into the seeds of a large pomegranate
and say pomegranate
there was a pomegranate

such a pomegranate:
and I swallow it

I show up only for myself
and those shows are accompanied by showers
of grasshoppers and crickets
from the low sky of tree canopies
They are actually the same creature

it's just that one lost its cry long ago
buried it inside the earth's breast
to guard it
and then forgot

Green on the eyes, red on the mouth
the other kept its cry within
and got a badminton racket
a racket like the one we used
to whack flying chafers, when we were children

and some would, after knocking the insects to the floor
halve them with the edge
thus ruining the racket
and pulling out its strings
but certainly not me

This morning the duck ate a pomegranate
Or, the duck lay that pomegranate yesterday
It was red
With a red beak and red tail
It was green
like a grasshopper, a cricket

red and green
like meat sitting in grass

It's Sunday today
all over the world

A standard day
like scrapes on knees
on elbows
calves and thighs of little girls
who play football
in a mine field
in grasses taller than their waists

In love, everything is the wrong way around   35
To break up means to begin
and to leave is — to come

To come to your senses on Thursday:
slap and embrace yourself
Push yourself into a corner

Something strange happens in the throat
a tiny word has hatched

On Wednesday he said I have a gift for you
something to remind you of me
and handed me a jewelry box tied with rope
the key to the flat was on the rope

I didn't want to take the key so he taught me
how to break into his flat
using a credit card

I did put the necklace on
— the wrong way around, so I don't get mugged —
and went for a long walk

It was Thursday, a warm evening

It was a beautiful evening of composure

On Friday I changed the lock
to fit his key

SHE'LL WAIT FOR SOME TIME

In the beautiful lady's house
soap and brandy were made from the same herb
She gave you something for your migraine, but you lost it
Later we drove as if we were fingers of one hand
going through tall, yellow grass

She made the petal dessert from the roses in her garden
She said she didn't eat sweets
and served it in small Moroccan bowls

Your left hand is on the steering wheel
your right hand takes mine and puts it on the gear stick
you say do you want me to teach you to drive

Tall electricity towers by the road
shift faster and faster

She said everyone is born alone
I did once have a husband
As she shows us sofa covers
that she brought from Ethiopia, the sun cracks
on crimson creases

Her house is as beautiful as a museum

Now your hand is on my thigh
I say don't mess around with me
If you were to teach me anything
someone will get seriously hurt

I imagine her beneath a bed's canopy
reaching out
but no one's there

She is going to Paris soon
the transport will be on strike
so the passengers will remain at the airport

She'll wait for some time to get to
where they are headed
time will seem limitless
but it won't be

The skin on your neck is fragrant

When it's touched with the lower lip
it stays pressed down

Don't look at me, keep your eyes on the road

All the roads bend before us
melted into a long, yellow beam

A LOCK OF HAIR

A forest sprouted, deciduous
from a lock of hair I snipped
tiny leaves fell out of the slit

Asleep you tell me the loveliest words
which you don't recall in the morning

Something like, I would like my spine to merge
with the line that separates the land and the sea
so my skin becomes the beach

And instead of the sun, you walk across me

Or perhaps I dreamed this, and you were awake
watching me smile in my sleep

I took the scissors and placed them in your hand

There was never anything but you

You watched me as I, dreaming
cut my hair with your hand

A lock of hair between the scissor edges
my tongue between your lips

A lock of golden hair fell on the floor

As I lay on your back
I weigh like the sun

THEN I WOKE UP TO CHECK IF YOU WERE STILL ALIVE

I dreamt that god came for you
he looked like your father
you said, oh please not you

he left and came back with the devil
the devil looked like my father
not you too, you said, not yet

none of us here believes in you

I woke up to check if you were still alive
put my hand under your nose to check if you were breathing

you had a bead of sweat on the tuft of hair above your ear
and slept, like a child

you were saying something in your sleep
something nice, which I don't remember

THE EYELIDS OF THE LONGSIGHTED

I coughed up a bird and it sung
A fat tree branched out of its beak

My uterus is a teapot with one ear
my liver is a golden goose

Reality cannot touch them

I am ill, but in high spirits
my eyes glisten and close
slower than usual

When you come over, don't bring medicine
This sickness is not to be cured

Inside my void
there is a bigger void
that makes you eternal

*

When you get close
leave the axe outside
you don't need it

*

This morning at the stream I saw
boys catching fish
bare handed

They fold their palms
like the longsighted fold their eyelids
and fish jump like butterflies

land on their plate

all of it happens as part of the game
the light dulls the eyes of the fish

a fish happens then a leap
and then comes the end of the fish

.

I have seen hundreds of boys and thousands of fish
as they play fishing with golden hoops
The boys lift the hoops up to the sky to catch
glints of sun
fish pass through them like half moons

That is how boys are full of youth and sleep
and the fish are full of light and leaps

The boys are so full of fish

Oh sun, you blinding all–seeing migraine
cruel and fair
that makes us multiply and die
one with another
one in another

the hoops we carry in our hands
are your shape
to which we pray

Today the crown of my head is heavy and warm

Witnessed from the ground, melted snow
gathers tiny locks of my hair
into small wreaths

Witnessed from the sky
it's a body shining in the snow
like a forest fire

The hoop stretches
placed around the heart so it doesn't crack
from its own expansion

Flocks of geese
fly toward the sun
for thousands of years

FISH

He tells me: this is how to catch fish
You put your palms together so they form a small boat
and then you cry into that plate

Fish is cleaned by opening its skin
with the knife's tongue
you take out the organs and place them on the table

Then you place a hook in each of your wounds
The wounds are already there
that's the whole point

You make sure that the oven is hotter than the sun
and you quickly put the fish inside

Fish must be cooked quickly
otherwise it'll forget that it is fish

While the fish is cooking
keep your gaze in the tray
and keep telling the tray you are fish

you are fish
you are fish

WHOEVER THOUGHT, WAS WRONG

Whoever thought that he wasn't ready, should know:
he was the readiest of all, sharpened the knife and kept
the fire going
until he lay the knife by the stove
and left
He no longer had to seek solitude
because solitude had moved into his teeth
and sat there, following wherever he went

Whoever thought he was ready, was wrong
She hopped from one rock to the next, remembering
short childhood episodes
like at the coast when she tripped over and grazed her
knee
while running, hot, to get a drink of water
she got up and carried on
with a clenched jaw

What happens on holidays, didn't happen
That's why every wound felt less deep
while traveling

This escape is her skin
This solitude is his safe friend
Whoever thought that he could not be the tooth inside
her wound
which closes all her memory holes
so that neither life nor pain can get out

And whoever thought that she had not entirely
transformed into his house
overgrown him with her hands, hair, and legs

That one had not heard the quiet echoes of a blow
of one stone against another
had not witnessed the slow, eternal waiting
of a forgotten knife

HOW WE LEFT THE BIRD

That crow was the first days of infatuation
In its beak it carried flowers and wrong assumptions
While departing we threw stones at it
We wanted to lose it, but keep its roses
We would gift them to each other
for important anniversaries

A hedge stormed out of clouds
Ants crawled through shoe soles

We crowned its memory
and gave it a special place in the park
The crow became a monument to the crow
and in the puddles, where it had hopped around
in the reflections of our insecure faces
one occasionally sees the logic of the claw
imprinted into our soft flesh

Ever since we shooed it away
it flies over each couple that walks down the street

It lets them know
that they're ordinary, tectonic
that they'll always be tiny and below
in comparison with its love

A type of dislocation follows us too
vibrates in the desperation of our desire
that each beginning really does eventually end
and that which precedes the beginning, begins

It greets the earth from a black cloud:
do you have any more walnuts?

I am hungry
for anyone's attention
like a firecracker and a fire extinguisher

'90S HAIRSTYLES

Every one of us is visible

That is what defines a person—
—how long one can bear
their own exposure

I tell you this, my legs half-hairy
as I eat a pear
and am enough for myself

I cough out the remains
of what I had dreamed of you
and declare them almost irrelevant

You breathe like a golden clock
left on the grass in springtime

*

It can be said that I trust you
Still I dreamed
that humanity is '90s hairstyles
a nostalgic supplement
which never outdoes the original
I am not referring to our nineties
I am referring to the Rachel and grunge
the teenage years we couldn't have

The comforting depictions of such youths
we watched on TV
playacting the actors' moves
and their clothes

I dreamed of all the ugly things
blade-nails and the flexibility
of interest rates

You take the lid off the lipstick and twist
A cut emerges out of it
instead of a kiss

*

We could have everything
speak in perfectly simple sentences
Be completely bare
freshly birthed humans
for whom the loss of shelter
is not a loss of dignity

You're as silent as the rust
on the toothed house
which we once drove by

*

I was born with large fists
and small teeth
the granddaughter of a builder
and a construction worker

I came into the world
hanging by the neck on the umbilical cord
and survived

My first work was
a failed suicide attempt

My first victory was
the victory over my death

Happiness poured into me afterward
through an open fontanelle

When love sung me a first lullaby
and then closed me

*

I buried my first period
into the foundations of a house
and it immediately collapsed

*

I was good once

Fed a stranger's dog
stroked a nobody's cat
moved to someone else's country twice

All those countries are now your countries
All that love is now your love
All that silence is yours

I MISS THE SMELL OF PLANT ROOTS

If mud were to appear under my feet
I would press down harder into the soil
my two axis
I stretch up high like an upturned dowsing rod

My skeleton is a tuning fork of the underground
and my arms bring only bad news

*

If mud were to flood cities
I would bend my back with my thumb and forefinger
and from the double fold of the ground
I'd pull out a pearl

My body is a bridge
upon which sleeps
a smaller bridge

*

The fish are dry in the stream
scales sharp, immobile they yawn eternally
sucking in the sun
or emitting the stream's song
fighting to get a word into their body
like a cashier who's fed up

Delaying is a bullet and a corkscrew
The July landscape is pointillism
with a fish-shaped hole on the belly

A pearly funeral goes on in the stream
The fish are lined up as if in a tin

Prophetically, alongside each other
they stretch their rubber eyes
into daisies without petals

The pearls
one by one
we lay them inside the fish mouths

*

All day
we will lay by the motionless scales
and pretend the sea doesn't exist

At midnight, we will swim upstream
and spit out the pearl before the shell

THE HOUSE

I lay my fingers on your closed eyelids
it's better when I see nothing, you say
there is no darkness or light in nothingness
everything seems human, as if you're my house

We had planned so much, but now the day is open
like a well-lit, abandoned train station
fronted by a swept street

That is why I plaster holes with my hands
careful that, in summer, wasps don't nest inside the
heart
as I fill those voids with love:

occasional eruptions, bits of resistance
several past lives that are easy to forget
five, six failed years full of experiments
and then periods of growth
short but stable
like a chubby hamster or a two-year marriage
and you weren't bad either

at first too good to win by cheating
later too proud to ask for what is yours
and so you found yourself alone
on the main square
with no one to blame
or owe

We counted on many things today
Planned a trip to the woods, and it rained

By day, the house is a cold wall
in front of which I left homemade bread
to cool down

The house is, by night, when you smile in your sleep
and everything lights up

WAITING

the body stores more memory than world history
history has a golden potato

love cannot save the world
love cannot even save those who love

the body lays in the ground, buried
the body of the ground waits below our feet

it is still in the core of history—nothing grows and nothing
walks

here it was that we don't have any more time to wait for the
end of the world

Aubade is a bison
Opening its horns like a water lily
and water is the dew evaporating in the movement of
the neck
upward
This mist gathers in the narrow
raised layer of fur that traces the spine
like a white deer following the traffic
when it snows
White lotus petals

or
white blood cells like pearl strings
that hang from the rooftops when it's cold
Aubade breath charges and races in its short
arrow flight
possibly like the life of a white rabbit
and other white animals

Aubade: it is the only brown thing on the horizon

Everything else is white, everywhere
wherever the small shotgun of the eye
covered with the frost's thin membrane
can form a trapeze
The only brown is a tree with four roots
and two branches

I don't know why, the aubade

reminded me of a juggler
who waits for the green light
at a crossing
Then starts to hurl up into the air
dusty tennis balls
sphere by sphere
like large, much too perfect walnuts
thump
If only one would fall onto the wet road
it would roll under the cars
that wait for the signal to change
and the day would be impoverished

This way, there is no mistake
No mud on the hands

My love is
a hunter that aims
for the empty space between the horns

To admire a bee, it awakens too early
and circles the dark alone
Instead of pollen, it collects the shimmer of the
sleeping balcony's fence so smooth that it appears
that the water runs down it
This surface sticks to its legs
as if it had stepped in honey
and it falls on the floor and stops:
this happens to me every morning

To admire a fish, it had gotten itself hooked knowingly
placed upon it by the fingers of the large, round sun
The fleshy, rough thumb and forefinger
flattened its mouth into an oval wound
and planted in it a rhetorical question

This wound doesn't hurt, you were born with it

To celebrate in darkness the sarcasm of a Monday
the calendar in which every animal looks alike
each stomach alike
a beak is on a giraffe
a sphere at a market place

To scrape off one's skin
to scan it in a park
and e-mail it to yourself

To do something new, unexpected
Maybe spilling apple juice

AMPHORA

To cover yourself in ashes
what a joyful thought after a century of sleep
inside an amphora
under a weight of heavy joy
Heavy, because waiting
to burst like a chestnut in an oven
and lay with a belly torn apart
and only then begin to dream

To dream of a budding olive
a bruise on the sky's thigh that the crow
pulled out of its own nest with its beak
thread by thread
until there was nothing left
except a dream about skinniness

and peace, reduction
a ceramic back
a door

To appear in the sun's apron
As if floating in an overgrown carriage
To rise up into a pillar that radiates from
the mouth of a bowl

An ordinary wooden bowl—
—the pit of our greeting is hard
and limp is its pose

To open your eyes
Invite an army to occupy the town
and place your forehead into a hollow
the inside of a joint

NITROGLYCERINE

You cannot heal a wound 65
unless you clean it first

*

You gather the cold into a lake
under which collar bones join
until your voice is strengthened
and it becomes
an echo in a cave
ready only to repeat
what was already said

When you achieve such roughness
it appears that water is dripping into the wound

*

This was the state they had in mind
when they came up with the expression
to be coolheaded

You breathe in

the wasteland of spring:
through the snow this winter
drag the tail ends of spring
like a drunken swallow

You breathe out

this time a little harder
it gets harder each time
after things
are named by you

*

A wound cannot be cleaned
with water
because it was inflicted
by a hard tongue
that laps water

the wound is all water too

The tongue sits inside a cave
that echoes with desire
to possess water

Nitroglycerine
carbon monoxide

A flat fire, drawn on the wall
in order to ornamentally
celebrate the difference

*

No one with a wound
can clean it

Those who don't have it
can't see it

If we meet
show me a wound

Tell me
my wound

doesn't hurt

and in it I will
see
my own wound

That's how I will come to love you

KINDNESS SEPARATES NIGHT FROM DAY

She keeps two dogs in the garden — mutts
of who knows how many breeds
Behind the house, the pomegranate shrub resembles a
wound
made by a lack of grooming
shampooing, care

I hear her yelling at him every day
screeching like a gray-haired bird and then, all too
humanly
weeping from the throat
When I prick my ears to hear her
as if through water
you've ruined my life and I have no one because of you
and the barking of the dog
but you'll see, one day when I'm gone
whose blood you'll leach off then

and I don't know if she's speaking to the husband
treating him like a dog
or the dog, treating him like a husband

I am sure that love divides a pet dog from a stray
just like kindness separates night from day
and I am ever more convinced that nothing worth
mentioning
separates humanity from other animals

Nothing tangible is visible in the dark, the pomegranate
shrub
seems to flood fast through its fur
Pomegranate fruit are polyps

that form on the neck where the chain digs in
and they peep out from under the fur
I am unsure if it's death rushing through the skin
or life breaking through the chain

69

One especially cold winter
She slipped on the frozen path when feeding the dogs
and broke her leg

I dreamed that she had finally died
and stopped torturing herself and the dogs
that the frost had settled and covered the pomegranates
the leg, and the polyps

I dreamed that I came with a saw, cut their chains

and liberated hundreds of her dogs who
alive and dead
finally left

they left on the path
that leads out of the courtyard
to eat her sadness and lick her wounds

THE TIME OF A LONG RECOVERY

We have come to an age where maturity
has nothing to do with age:
birds communicate by movements that
mimic the trajectory
of celestial bodies
Frogs sail the seas
using their smooth neck membranes
like sails
Seven days of solitude went like this:
On the first day, I didn't even realize I was alone

On the second day, life went on as usual
was ordinary
I ate nothing
and slept little
I made a soup out of your shirt
in case any visitors came knocking on the door
I cleaned the windows with it in the end
better that than throwing
a random insult at the door
a door that no one comes through because I forbade it
a door that is locked
sewn into the warm wall of my stomach
a swallowed hedgehog nest

On the third day, I realized I was alone
The fish got frightened and gathered together
Held a meeting in which they decided
that from tomorrow they'd live like silver bats
Flying towards the light, closing their eyes
and count the days with the sensors they have in their
throats

I decided to remain alone
and embrace my new state
as the time of a long recovery

I don't remember the fourth day

I remember the fifth day well
but I'd rather not talk about it

On the sixth day, I decided:
I will be alone

And really, on the seventh day
It's as if ice cracks in my knees
in my thanks
in the ankles of the spider—me
which resembles a dog
in the teeth of the fox—me
which resembles a wolf

IMMORTAL

My greatest power is
that I sometimes wish I wasn't here
So that, when I am, then I really am here

You should visit me
see that I am well
I plant herbs in pots at home
poisonous and healing like mother's love

In the yard — weeds
resilient and inaudible like father's love

Everything that's mine belongs to me
and nothing else
That's why I can share everything with you
The night and the day

You're not dead
you're as immortal as the trend of bushy eyebrows
and morning coffee

Every now and then someone says you're not there —
— how come I see you in everyone's face?

Superstitions exist so we can blame ourselves
for things that happens to us, and are beyond our control
For example, you're making soup, stirring it with a knife
and two hours later, a pile of books falls on the foot
of someone for whom you set a plate on the table
This way you think it's your fault, rather than an accident
This is how you protect yourself, you're always prepared

Or, in contrast, they exist so that the things that happen
through your own fault, can be blamed on something
that is beyond your control
For instance, a black cat crosses your path
and two days later you buy a T-shirt you don't need
On the way home, you see it's ripped
has a crooked sleeve
Where was I? What was I doing? I was cursed
by that cat
and the knife took offense too

You always assign greater or lesser power to yourself
than you really have
and that is how you're safe, always able to choose to fight
    or flee
you can leave everything for tomorrow
You can say, for example, if we knew where we'd fall
we would never take off
Or, god said take care of yourself — I'll take care of you
That is how you're a pup with metal claws, you can say
someone will eventually save me

You have no major mistakes in life
You didn't achieve too much either
It's Tuesday, you're sitting in your room, eating the
cursed soup
and wearing the crooked T-shirt

ICELAND

I'll go to live in Iceland
like a flock of birds, two bundles of hay
that walk around in the sun
until they faint, their skin
harnessed with soft reins
onto vertigo

I say: it's reliable
it doesn't mean: security

it means:
my body is tied
and I float like an amoeba
free
like a life buoy
without the person
that is drowning

The empty center
Is Iceland:
my need
to be warm
hurled into water

my desire
to see you
bombed to pieces
from my belly

my hands
hold binoculars
and watch me from the shore
in an explosion
that calls me

to forget my name

*

Iceland
The intention to become cold
To only have sterile thoughts
and utter only simple sentences
to be stranded onto a rock of wet salt
and eat bland oat meal

To wear thick woolen socks
renounce the closeness of people
and visit once a month
white foxes

I wish for an eternal winter
I would like the courtyard of my room
to become its empire
and for me to lay on its cushions

it would tell me how in its youth
it sat on the chests of young men
and stayed with them
until they ran
out of breath

*

I write to you from Iceland:
everything is white here
like the footage of clouds
through the airplane window
when I was coming to you

During the day, the sky seemed
as if it were the North Pole
the Earth wasn't visible

At night, the landing ground
looked like a web of stars

I don't mention brown details
I lie that it had snowed
I don't send the letter in the end
I don't start hating the world
I get under the covers naked
and I don't cry

*

Your core is tiny
ruddy smooth soft
tissue under a pile of knives

One white morning
I will pull the knives out one by one
like tent nails
and stab them into the foreheads of those
who'd exposed you

ABOUT SANDORF PASSAGE

Sandorf Passage publishes work that creates a prismatic perspective on what it means to live in a globalized world. It is a home to writing inspired by both conflict zones and the dangers of complacency. All Sandorf Passage titles share in common how the biggest and most important ideas are best explored in the most personal and intimate of spaces.